Crystals

Connor Dayton

PowerKiDS press™

New York

Published in 2007 by The Rosen Publishing Group, Inc.
29 East 21st Street, New York, NY 10010

First Edition

Editor: Jennifer Way
Book Design: Greg Tucker
Photo Researcher: Sam Cha

Photo Credits: All images Shutterstock.com.

Library of Congress Cataloging-in-Publication Data

Dayton, Connor.
  Crystals / Connor Dayton. — 1st ed.
      p. cm. — (Rocks and minerals)
  Includes bibliographical references and index.
  ISBN-13: 978-1-4042-3687-5 (lib. bdg.)
  ISBN-10: 1-4042-3687-2 (lib. bdg.)
  1. Crystals—Juvenile literature. 2. Crystal growth—Juvenile literature. 3. Rocks—Analysis—Juvenile literature. 4. Minerals—Analysis—Juvenile literature. I. Title.
  QD921.D29 2007
  548—dc22
                                                2006029631

Manufactured in the United States of America

Contents

What Are Crystals?

Crystals are solids in which the smallest pieces are all ordered in a pattern, or form. These pieces are **atoms**, **molecules**, and **ions**. A crystal's pattern takes the same shape in all directions. The way in which a crystal is held together is called its bond. You can find crystals in many of the rocks you see every day.

There are many ways to tell crystals apart. Each type of crystal has its own shape, size, and color. Each type of crystal is also made of its own special mix of **elements** or minerals.

This is a group of sulphur crystals. Sulphur is an element that is known for smelling like rotten eggs.

How Do Crystals Form?

Crystals form when **liquid** molecules make bonds that turn them into solid molecules. This is called crystallization. Many things help decide how liquid crystallizes. One of these things can be the **pressure** under which crystallization happens. It can also be the **chemistry** of the liquid molecule or how fast crystallization happens.

For example, water is made of the elements hydrogen and oxygen. When water cools ice crystals can form. The rate of cooling and the coldness of the air help decide the form the ice crystals will take. Ice crystals make up ice, snow, hail, and freezing rain.

Ice crystals can grow into many forms. These crystals have formed into a very thin sheet on a window.

Structure and Symmetry

Crystals are grouped by their structure and by their **symmetry**. Every crystal has a pattern in which its molecules are ordered. This is the crystal's structure. The crystal structure takes form from a point called the unit cell.

If you turn a crystal in different directions, you will see that from some views the crystal looks like it did before you turned it. This is called a crystal's symmetry.

Structure and symmetry both play a part in a crystal's **properties**. Crystals are also grouped by the type of bonds of which they are made.

Gypsum has a large, flat crystal structure. Two of gypsum's properties are its softness and the fact that it leaves a white mark when rubbed against something else.

Ionic Bonds

Ionic bonds are common chemical bonds that form between two ions. An ion is an atom that has an **electric** charge. This charge is either positive or **negative**. Ions are attracted, or drawn, to form bonds with ions of an unlike charge. Salt is an example of a crystal made of ionic bonds.

Crystals with ionic bonds often have many properties in common. They tend to be hard. They also need lots of heat before they will melt. When something melts, that shows that the bonds holding it together are breaking down.

Salt crystals are formed by the ionic bonding of the elements sodium and chlorine.

Covalent Bonds

Covalent bonds are the strongest chemical bonds. In covalent bonds, atoms share their **electrons**. This makes these bonds very hard to break.

Crystals made of covalent bonds have many things in common. They are often very hard. They need more heat to melt than do crystals with ionic bonds. Unlike some ionically bonded crystals, covalently bonded crystals do not dissolve in water. "Dissolve" means "to break down." Diamonds are made of covalent bonds. Diamonds are the hardest things on Earth.

Diamond crystals are made of covalent bonds. Because these bonds are so hard to break, diamonds have to be used to cut other diamonds!

Other Bonds

There are other bonds that can hold together crystals. Two of these are metallic bonds and van der Waals bonds. In a metallic bond, electrons are not very strongly bonded to their atoms. This lets the electrons bond with different atoms. Copper forms crystals with metallic bonds. This makes copper easy to shape or melt.

Van der Waals bonds are the least strong chemical bonds. They make crystals that are soft and break easily. Graphite is an example of a crystal with a van der Waals bond. It is so soft that it is used in pencil lead!

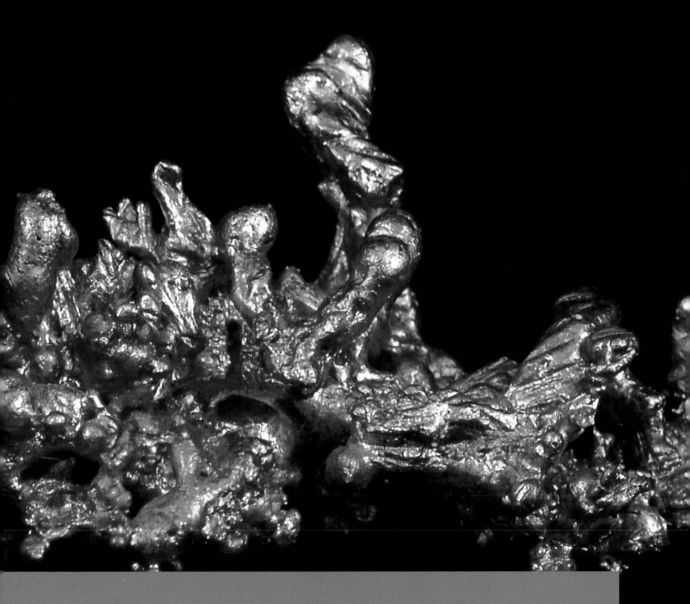

Copper crystals are held together by metallic bonds.
Copper is used for many things, such as pots and pans.

Monocrystals and Crystal Groupings

The size of crystals is also decided by the **conditions** under which the crystal is formed. These conditions are heat, pressure, and the amount of space in which the crystal is growing. If there is plenty of space and the right amount of heat and pressure, one large crystal can form. This is called a monocrystal.

Most of the time, conditions keep monocrystals from forming. Instead crystal groupings will form. Crystal groupings may grow around minerals or other matter. Matter might also get trapped in the crystal. Crystal groupings can be seen in the rocks you can find every day.

There are two crystal groupings in this rock. Calcite is the large, milky crystal in the middle. There are thinner, clear quartz crystals on the sides.

Quartz

Quartz is one of the most common kinds of crystal on Earth. It can be found in rocks just about everywhere. Quartz is made of the elements silicon and oxygen. Quartz crystals are held together by covalent bonds. This makes quartz very hard.

By itself, quartz is clear and colorless. It can be other colors if other minerals mix in during its formation. These colored quartzes sometimes have different names. For example, solid-colored black quartz is called onyx.

Quartz has many different uses. It is used in sandpaper. Quartz is even used to make watches tell time!

These clear, colorless quartz crystals do not have other minerals mixed in with them.

Geodes

Sometimes crystals grow in a pocket inside a rock. This kind of crystal formation is called a geode.

Geodes form when water carries minerals into a rock. The water **evaporates** and leaves the minerals behind. This is called a mineral deposit. Over time the minerals build up and crystals begin to form.

Geode crystals are most often different kinds of quartz. Sometimes this quartz is a purple color that is known as the gemstone amethyst. Geodes can be any size. Crystal Cave is one of the largest geodes. It is about the size of a van!

This geode is filled with clear quartz crystals. Other geodes may have amethyst or other colored quartz crystals in them.

Crystals Are Everywhere!

People have put crystals to many uses. They are used in **jewelry** because of the way they shine and catch the light. Some people believe that certain crystals can make sick people better. Crystals are also used in machines, such as clocks and radios.

The snow that falls in the winter is made of water crystals. Crystals also make up the sugar and the salt used to add taste to foods. There are crystals in many of the rocks in your backyard. Whether they are large or tiny, you can find different kinds of crystals everywhere you look.

Glossary

atoms (A-temz) The smallest parts of elements.

chemistry (KEH-mih-stree) The makeup of matter.

conditions (kun-DIH-shunz) The ways people or things are or the shape they are in.

electric (ih-LEK-trik) Having to do with power that produces light, heat, or movement.

electrons (ih-LEK-tronz) The parts of atoms that have a negative charge.

elements (EH-luh-ments) The basic matter of which all things are made.

evaporates (ih-VA-puh-rayts) Changes from a liquid to a gas.

ions (EYE-unz) Tiny pieces of charged matter.

jewelry (JOO-ul-ree) Objects worn for decoration that are made of special metals, such as gold and silver, and prized stones.

liquid (LIH-kwed) Matter that flows.

molecules (MAH-lih-kyoolz) The smallest bits of matter possible before they can be broken down into their basic parts.

negative (NEH-guh-tiv) Having a charge that is not positive.

pressure (PREH-shur) A force that pushes on something.

properties (PRAH-pur-teez) Things that describe something.

symmetry (SIH-muh-tree) Meaning that something is equal on all sides.

Index

Web Sites

Due to the changing nature of Internet links, PowerKids Press has developed an online list of Web sites related to the subject of this book. This site is updated regularly. Please use this link to access the list:

www.powerkidslinks.com/romi/cryst/